I0435913

MY UGLY

The Beginning of the Journey to My Beauty

FLOWER

authorHOUSE®

AuthorHouse™
1663 Liberty Drive
Bloomington, IN 47403
www.authorhouse.com
Phone: 1 (800) 839-8640

© *2016 Flower. All rights reserved.*

No part of this book may be reproduced, stored in a retrieval system, or transmitted by any means without the written permission of the author.

Published by AuthorHouse 02/23/2016

ISBN: 978-1-5049-8168-2 (sc)
ISBN: 978-1-5049-8167-5 (e)

Print information available on the last page.

Any people depicted in stock imagery provided by Thinkstock are models, and such images are being used for illustrative purposes only. Certain stock imagery © Thinkstock.

This book is printed on acid-free paper.

Because of the dynamic nature of the Internet, any web addresses or links contained in this book may have changed since publication and may no longer be valid. The views expressed in this work are solely those of the author and do not necessarily reflect the views of the publisher, and the publisher hereby disclaims any responsibility for them.

Contents

It's the summer of 2014 and I just finished a Cry Fest while running on the treadmill and watching motivational videos on YouTube; Lilou Mace's interview with Jack Canfield, Brian Johnson's Philosopher's Notes on Thresholds of the Mind by Bill Harris and finally, my favorite, a remarkable woman whom I met in person at a phenomenal, life changing communication seminar in San Diego. Her eyes marked my soul with a resounding, "Get with it girl and lets run together!" her name, Lisa Nichols. Now, as I watch her at Awesomeness Fest, I cry. I cry because I know what I have to do and it's going to hurt.

Do what? Share my ugly.

Why? Because, my ugly is what's been holding me back from living my truest dreams of success and personal fulfillment; I've tried "moving on" and "getting over it", but My Ugly is who I am and it's holding me down like an iron ball and chain. So, I'm ready to change that. I'm ready to put my past to work for me AND EVEN make it bless my future. I encourage you to do the same. I'm convinced that if I don't do this, then I'm thwarting your dreams as well, because without action on my part, I can't influence you to move through your inner pain in search of freedom. For too long I've tried to pretend that this "shit" doesn't exist, but pretending isn't serving me like a reality check would.

What is my ugly?

Warning: My Ugly is the raw, uncensored, true accounts of grotesque sexual abuse I've suffered and the horrific witness of intense violence to which I was exposed.

For the longest time I thought publishing my story would be to glorify evil, but then I realized how atrocities don't generally appeal to others as a celebration and therefore neither would my story to you, and if it does, God help you.

So, now I lay my ugly in the pages before you in hopes that you'll receives impetus to release the ugly of your own past, unlock the truest beauty within and soar. Even if only one person is touched and rescued from despair by reading this, then baring all my shame is worth it, because you're worth it. Read that again; YOU ARE WORTH IT; even if I'm the only one. That's what makes me write.

Along my journey, I've encountered people with even more arduous battles to overcome than my own. And my hope in writing this is to shed light on the treasures I've uncovered, and am still uncovering, in the process of crawling my way to freedom. Every priceless trait I've found along the way, you also have within you, whether you know it or not. By design, each of us has a power source to tap; an innate ability to persevere, evolve, and be made better by every challenge that besets us. We also have access to an immense personal reservoir of peace. No one can take these things away from us, for they only exist because we do.

As we sojourn through the relics of my past and I dig up treasures, I'll strive to put them to immediate and appropriate use. I hope you'll glean and do the same. Together, we'll build confidence, become more resilient and make a way where there seems to be no way. Let's get this journey started!

This book is dedicated first and foremost to my older sister, Azurdee. She endured much greater trauma than I, and she still did all she could to protect me, (and others).

Thank you Azure, I love you.

This book is also dedicated to every person who has ever felt worthless. If you can relate to abuse, whether on the giving or receiving end, or as one who turned a blind eye, this book is for you. Sometimes things in life, layer by layer, mislead us to false beliefs in ourselves and it's my desire to help remove those masks and uncover the truth, because you're worth it. Every ache in my heart, as I relive this agony, reminds me that you're totally worth it.

I hope you'll join me in discovering the precious wonder that you are.

Brief Overview:

If only I knew then, what I know now...

Thanks to hindsight, I've since learned that wherever you go, there you are, but as a young adolescent, I didn't understand this universal law and began running away in attempts to save myself, or so I thought. But, what I'd endured up to that point was brutal.

Name Changes

For every single name I thought of using for the villain of my past, I was consumed with worry that readers might connect the name I chose to painful memories of their own. Then I considered calling him Monster, or some other evil thing, but compassion and forgiveness wouldn't allow it. Finally, after much prayer and deliberation I felt instructed to look up his name's meaning and use that. The meaning utterly shocked me! I told God I could not use it! But, the feeling persisted that I was supposed to, so I decided to trust that God has a purpose and a plan for using Him as my villain.

Chapter 1

Who's Your Daddy?

Mom and I were driving on a winding country road and I began to tell her about some memories I had of myself as a baby in the hospital. I thought I must've seen pictures, but she said there were none. I was born prematurely, at 7 months along, and placed in intensive care, struggling to survive due to my supposed father beating her. I recall being up in the corner of the room looking down at myself in a glass coffin, like Snow White, turns out it was an incubator. I had tubes and wires coming out of my head and limbs. Some were connected to a bulky, square, beeping machine with colored, blinking lights. Others were hooked to bags of fluid. In one out of body experience, there was an older, gray haired, peaceful woman holding me tenderly in a rocking chair. I can still hear the soft, soothing hum of her voice as she sang to me. My mom said she was a hospital volunteer to visit babies. In another experience, I was with a shorter, dark haired woman that held me steadily, flat on my back. Mom said that was my Aunt from whom I frequently received blood transfusions, since I didn't match the blood type of either parent. That is why I call this dad my supposed father. I even felt compelled to ask if he was really my father and if she was my mother. Mom seemed astonished by my story and my inquiries and she insisted they were both my parents.

For years, mom was with a man whom I thought was my dad. I remember some pretty amazing times; like snuggling on the couch with daddy, reading Puss in Boots as a family, which I seem to recall always being filled with wild musing's about pussy. Haha! Getting ice cream after school, sneaking raw hamburger meat when mom was cooking, and accidentally stealing a Mickey Mouse straw, because it said FREE! Actually, it said "Buy one, get one FREE! But all I could read at the time was GET and FREE! So I got one! Regrettably, my aunt made me take it back. She must have told me a really good reason, cuz I was actually satisfied to do the right thing. To my surprise, she paid for it and we got two! I also remember a couple of hostile feuds between mom and daddy, but they were nothing compared to what I would eventually witness.

A memory that bothered me for years was a time when I tried unplugging a clock and its protective cover came off and shocked me. I received one hellacious fucked up jolt from that thing! But, not realizing the actual dangers of it, I tried convincing my younger sister to touch it so that I could watch her experience, and understand what happened to me. Everything was like an experiment to me.

Thankfully she screamed like the dickens and mom came in to the rescue. Sorry sis!

As a child, I suffered from recurrent ear infections, eventually requiring surgery to have my tonsils and adenoids removed. I wasn't sure what this meant, but I wasn't sticking around to find out! And, I certainly didn't trust the creeps in white coats! So, like a lab rat I ran straightaway into the nearest elevator. Of course, I was soon caught, had the surgery and everything was fine, especially the ice cream diet afterward...but I let them know I wasn't going down without a fight!

A few other amusing memories that occurred before I found myself cowering in tumultuous chaos were things like; hiding in the pantry eating dry dog food because I loved it, drinking warm sugar water from a baby bottle on the couch while watching the movie Jaws, picking my nose with a butter knife, witnessing the downpour of a magnificent rainstorm from the front screen door, our family taking music trips for daddy's band to play at various events, playing with a little girl named Running Water, and finally, being caught playing Mork and Mindy in the closet with a cousin, when we were both 4. Let me tell you about that game...for some reason both characters, Mork and Mindy, had to be naked, in a dark room, with one sitting on the back of the other, who was curled up like an egg, (in order for the egg to hatch of course). I'm not sure why, but, that's how the game was played. And so, he and I were found naked, one sitting on the other in the dark, on the closet floor. And no, we NEVER lived it down!

When mother told me that daddy wasn't really mine, I was immediately given the choice to go live with my supposed real father who was also father to my sister Azurdee that already lived with him. I loved daddy and felt deeply connected to him. I didn't want to go, and daddy didn't want me to leave either, so I declined.

But then Mom said, "It'll be like a vacation...

If you don't like it, you can always come back home."
so I went.

Let's assume feeling unheard was mask #1. My mission now is to be an eloquent communicator and take responsibility in being understood.

And, so the next five years ensued the most ugly my life has ever known. Thankfully it was limited to only 5 years or maybe I'd be more crazy than I am.

I'm not really sure where to begin with my story and I'm tempted to skirt edges, sugar coat and hide things just to spare myself some shame and disgrace. But doing that will only serve me as well as it has in the past, which is not at all.

I don't recall the events in order, and I'm sure there are some that I'll never remember, so I'm just going to jump right in and share my most shameful, humiliating ordeal that I believe was also my first molestation experience. This memory was completely blocked from my mind until 2009 when I was in my mid 30's, and it continued to disturb me for years after that. I just remembered pain and crying. Its presence left me moody, distraught, and aggravated. I felt dirty, gross and suicidal, but I could tell no one. The memory persisted. It started to make me feel crazy and out of control, even waking me in the night with full blown panic attacks. I knew I had to go back and relive the moment in order to move on with my life, but the mere thought of it made me so anxious that I couldn't do it and I was too ashamed to seek help. I hated even thinking about it, but it wouldn't let me be. It just grew in seducing power.

Chapter 2

Debauchery

Wait! Can I be totally candid with you?

Before we transcend the depths of my personal hell, I'd like you to get to know a little more about the kind of child that I was before my eventual, unconscious retreat.

This story is an absolute must tell! In fact, it's blackmail worthy! But too bad, so sad for you, only my mama was able to use it, and she forfeited that right, THANK GOD!

Maybe I learned about digestion at school, I'm not sure, but one day I went potty; it stunk and this really bothered me, so I asked, "Mom, what's poop?" And she said, "Well honey, it's everything you eat that your body doesn't need anymore." Hmm, I thought to myself, well then, from now on I'm only going to eat what I like, then, my poop will smell good. Some days later I went potty again and to my surprise it still stunk! I sat there on the throne, thinking... I just had to figure it out, and then I recalled how some things I like to eat smell badly, like hard boiled eggs and broccoli, so I figured this must be like that and then it dawned on me...it was time to experiment. Yep, you see where this is going... I dutifully wiped my bottom and discarded the paper in the waste receptacle, instead of the toilet, so as to not defile my ample, brown specimen...I stood up valiantly, turned around and stared into the great white abyss...there, all alone, floated my turd. The odor made me grimace and I shook my head. Glancing down at my folded hands, placed gracefully in front of me, I slowly held up one dutiful finger. Then carefully leaning over the toilet, I bent downward and poked the turd swiftly, trying not to get any toilet water get on me. Finally, a smidgen of poop adorned my fingertip.

And now for the moment of truth.

Staring at my finger, I forced my tongue out. Barely grazing it was more than enough to make my mouth water and make me jerk my head back! Rushing to the sink I washed my tongue and hands. Then I ran to my mother to be vindicated! "Mom! You said poop was everything I ate!" I contested. "It is." She declared, looking dismayed. Then I adamantly informed her, "Well, I only ate the things I like!" Bewildered, she inquired further with a nod of her head, "Yeah?" So emphatically I carried on, "Yeah! Last time I went poop it stunk, so then, I only ate the things I like and it still stinks! then I thought it was like eggs or broccoli cuz I like those things and they stink and…." Meanwhile her eyes became large and concerned and her head began to shake a slow, concerning no, but I carried on. "…and I tasted it and it tastes like…like…" "Like what?" She asked distressingly. "Like POOP!" I exclaimed abhorrently.

And so, there you have it. If I ever say something tastes like shit, I ain't lyin'!

And Now We Enter The Abyss

Like I said, in 2009, I began having a memory…

After a mortifying discussion with a relative at a memorial service, I was left completely speechless. I sat there numb, unemotional, and completely dumb-stricken as she described an incident that would later serve as a catalyst of freedom from such horrific torment.

Later that night I drove home, tears fell down my face as the conversation lingered in my mind. I cried for the suffering she endured at the hands of the same individual that I had fallen prey to. That poor woman, I thought to myself, she doesn't know what a beautiful princess and extravagant queen she was designed to be, nor did her abuser know what lofty kingship was his lost identity.

And as I drove, the memory began. I saw myself cringing on the floor, face-down. I felt the sensation of dog slobber drip down the side of my neck. The memory was so vivid that it caused me to cinch my right shoulder to stop the dribble.

Could this be real? I asked myself. And then the feeling of its utter reality brought streams of tears to the point that I began driving by brail on the long desert highway.

The memory continued to haunt me until 2014 and as I said earlier, it was slowly crippling me. I was too ashamed to tell anyone for fear that they would reject me and be repulsed by my presence. Finally, after much debate within myself, I decided to look at the situation differently, to reverse it, as if someone else were telling me that it happened to them. Would I say, "Oh fuck! You should just kill yourself. That's disgusting! Get away from me!" Absolutely not! I would never respond that way! Nor would I even think it! Afterall, someone did tell me it happened to them, that's what started this whole thing in the first place! But I didn't shun them, I just sat there in disbelief, grief stricken. Yet I couldn't stop assuming that people would treat me with contempt, because I was different. I was ugly, I was dirty, I was gross.

And worst of all, it was all my fault. Eventually, I determined that no one, or very few, would actually revile me, and if they did, "Fuck em'!" it was this mindful resolution that gave me the courage to tell my therapist and a trusted friend. They comforted me and supported my decision to revisit the event in its entirety in order to bring closure. Consequently, I also decided I would not kill myself if the event was indeed real. Instead, I would lean heavily on friends and on strong doses of psychiatric drugs to get me through, even though I don't even like taking Tylenol. I'd use the meds until I was able to deal with the dread in real life.

It took months to gain the courage to revisit the disturbing memory in its totality, but I am not at liberty to share it in this book due to publishing legalities.

There's no doubt in my mind that this is the circumstance that first taught me how to run away inside myself; to hide and not be in reality. I believe that in psychology it's called dissociation and later in life it became quite an art for me. Let's call this hiding mask #2. Coming out of my shell is a little scary, actually, it's hard as hell, but I'm determined because it's necessary in order to fulfill my heart's greatest desire and live.

Chapter 3

It's all Fun and Games Until Someone Gets Hurt...

When I went to live with my sister Azurdee, dad, stepmom and stepbrother, for some reason I had no recollection of the incident with Christ and the dog.

At first we lived at a campground or mobile home park on a hillside, near a riverbed. Our parents struggled to get along, but there were some hysterical times too! One night dad was running around the trailer in his underwear, farting. Stepmom flicked a lighter at his butt as he passed by. Suddenly a flame burst out of his rear end and he squealed! They hurried to put it out and we all roared with laughed, hiding our faces from the gruesome smell.

Us kids often played hide and seek in the riverbed with other kids. It was my favorite game because it gave me time to myself. The most outrageous thing we did was slide down a hill on a sheet of corrugated metal that most likely came from the roof of a nearby shed. The 3 of us discussed how to guide the 'sled' down the hill and then we all jumped on in train formation. The brown grass was much slicker than expected and we soon sped out of control, heading straight for a big thorny bush! Despite our best maneuvering antics, we crashed right into it! All of us were injured, scraped up and banged.

One day stepbrother and I were in a vacant shed. He tried convincing me to take my clothes off. It seemed like I hadn't done something like that in a long time, so it felt awkward and I hesitated. Thankfully, my sister walked in and the atmosphere changed, so he offered us cigarettes instead, which tasted disgusting.

Eventually we moved several hours away. Our new home was nice and spacious and the promise of a bright and beautiful future was upon us.

What Good is a Teddy Bear When You Need a Gun?

At first, Azure and I slept on the living room floor because our bedroom wasn't set up yet. And on this particular night, everyone was asleep, but I couldn't because of some earlier quarreling between our folks. I lay there, baffled at how everyone could rest at ease as if nothing had happened. After what felt like eternity, dad's snoring became like a lullaby and I finally dozed off, only to be startled by a hand sliding into my pants. I screamed and faster than my eyes could adjust, Azure bolted up and grabbed a loaded 22 rifle leaning on a nearby table.

Time stood still.

Aiming just inches from his face, she looked deep in his eyes and pulled the trigger.

It misfired.

And I don't remember anything else from that night.

We hadn't lived there long, when the school bus dropped me off and I started to skip home. I saw the cutest dog & wandered towards it. To my surprise, its owner, a young, nicely dressed, most unpleasant man confronted me about my parents. In a nutshell, he wanted me to relay the message that he wasn't going to put up with their kind, but of course, I never said a word.

On the plus side, while living here, we got horses and us girls got to name them.

They were beautiful and we dubbed them, Shadow and No One; two very fitting names from the mouths of 2 forgotten girls. Forgotten = mask #3, but let's replace that lie with being thought of fondly, being cared for and remembered.

I'm sure it was NOT intended for us to feel forgotten. In fact, I remember a time when Dad and Azurdee were teaching me how to bathe the horses. I kept worrying that I'd make a mistake and get yelled at. Then I bent down near the rear of the horse and got whacked in the head when it flinched to shoo flies. Tammy said it was the horse's ankle that got me and that I was lucky it wasn't the hoof. Dad let out an exasperating sigh, but he didn't say a word.

One day when I came home from school, Christ asked if I wanted to jump on the bed. No one else was home and I felt uneasy, but eager to play, so I agreed. He held my hands while I jumped high in the air. My hair almost touched the ceiling! I laughed so hard! Then all at once I got really tired and fell asleep; turns out I had asthma, which wasn't discovered until my 30's. I woke up later but remained frozen, pretending to be asleep so that nothing further would be expected of me. Suddenly a sensation took my breath away. It felt good, though simultaneously I felt bad. When he left, I locked myself in the bathroom and took a shower. I was crying and scrubbing myself when my sister broke in and ask me that question I do not want to hear. I shook my head. She swore he'd never do that again and that she'd always be home before me. She had to skip school to accomplish this, but she didn't care. Azurdee would do anything to protect me. Some days later I came home and found them both in a trailer; she had told him to leave me alone and touch her instead. She looked sad and I hesitated to leave, as if feeling compelled to join them, but my joining would not save her, so I wandered off for a long walk, finding solitude among the grassy hills and lush trees.

Upon arriving back home, I could hear dad and stepmom fighting. Azure and Christ were manic trying to stop them. **They were very familiar with all of this chaos and I felt sad for them.**

Chapter 4

Hoping for a Friendly Face

I guess the sweet home was an example of biting off more than could be chewed, financially speaking, because we moved again; this time onto private property out in the country. **Nice and secluded where evil prevailed and engulfed our entire world.** On a happy note, my step brother was often gone to his dad's.

Our new home was small. A one bedroom house atop an oak tree covered hillside. We still had the trailer and camper shell and used them for our bedrooms. When Azurdee and I were walking home from the bus stop, along a half mile country dirt road, we could smell dinner cooking as we approached the house and we were hungry! It was gonna be a good night. We followed our noses into the kitchen and there stood dad, holding stepmom in the air, choking her! His face was beat red all the way to the top of his balding scalp and her face was grayish purple and blood was dripping from one of her nostril's and eyes! Without hesitating, Azure smacked dad in the arm with all her might and Stepmom fell to the floor in a lifeless heap. Dad twisted and surged after us with eyes that knew no mercy! Azure yanked me and screamed, "Run!" Shaken out of my frozen state of terror, I ran after her. I looked back and saw Dad grab a bat. He threw it, hitting me in the ankle and tripping me up! We came to a barbed wire fence and before I knew it, Azure grabbed me by the waist of my pants and the back of my shirt and threw me over! We both got scraped up, but kept running down the hill. Finally we came to a trailer with several dogs. No one was home. After waiting around, hoping for a friendly face, but fearing another enraged lunatic, we headed back toward home, finding refuge in an old truck down the hill from our house. **Mask #5 is scared, but I'm not afraid anymore. I don't need to be because I've found a safe haven within myself.**

I sit here now, in this moment crying and trembling deeply for those 2 little girls, and for both of my "mothers". My head, face and body are tingling uncontrollably. I'm dizzy. I need help. I hate this! "Oh God, please don't let me pass out!" In a panic I pace the floor and fall to my knees, throwing my hands in the air, my Spirit groans as I cry out in tongues I don't even know, yet somehow I'm intricately connected to its meaning.

Alas, I'm rescued, comforted and even healed retroactively through the remembrance of every act of human kindness I've ever known. Can you feel it? Goodness does prevail.

Somehow the place with the dogs became a safe haven for me, but sadly, not for my sister. I loved caring for the dogs; grooming them, washing their food and water dishes, playing with them and their puppies, and just hanging around talking to them. Being with them brought a peace I can't explain.

An Author in the Making

At one elementary school I briefly attended, a boy came up to me and humped my leg. Then, to my astonishment, his sister, who was standing right next to me asked if I liked him. I paused and said, "No, he's weird." And wham! She punched me in the stomach, knocking the wind out of me. Bewildered and frazzled, I went and sat under a tree. Shortly thereafter, a group of girls came and invited me to play. Fearing it to be a trap to more pain, I declined as sweetly as I could, hoping not to hurt their feelings or upset them.

It seemed at any school I attended, I just felt lost. I often fall asleep in class, having to miss recess for it, but I didn't seem to mind. I don't think I knew what I was missing. One time I dreamed that I was in the restroom and when I woke up, I was peeing at my desk. The funny thing is, I don't remember feeling any more embarrassed than I already always seemed to feel. **Bringing us to mask #4, I'll call it disconcerted, because I was lost and disconnected from the world. But I'm not anymore. I've found myself. I'm regaining my composure and I'm making my way in the world come hell or high water.**

In the country, I went to a new school and I loved it, though I still slept in class and rarely turned in homework. As I got older, I eventually resorted to cheating because I had no idea what was going on. I wasn't intending to do wrong; I was just trying to keep up.

To this day, I'm not sure why, but a teacher's aide said I'd be an author someday and it stuck with me ever since. Maybe that's why this was my favorite school; someone believed in me, long before I believed in myself.

Chapter 5

Waiting on a Savior

Now let's go back to those precious girls waiting on a savior. Hours passed and we woke up in the truck under a blanket of darkness and dad's voice, calling, pleading, "Azure! Flower! I'm sorry! Please come home!" He sounded so broken, so hurt, so sorry. I wanted to be happy. I wanted to believe him, I wanted to trust him and I wondered if Azure did too. I just wanted everything to be ok. Then I remembered we didn't even know if stepmom was alive and that scared me. My tummy trembled with fear and hunger pangs. I trusted Azure to know when it was safe to go back. She woke me later to go to our room, which was actually the little trailer on the side of the house. The trailer's electrical wasn't grounded, so you'd get quite the shock when touching two metals, (I received more than my share of jolts from that thing), but there were pleasant times too, like drawing the trees I could see outside the window and trying to draw the animals.

Anyway, the next morning we rose early and walked to the bus stop before the sun was even up. After Azure's bus left, I slept in the bushes for about 45 minutes until mine arrived; still dressed in the same clothes as the day before, no shower, no breakfast, no homework, and no dinner the night before. I still remember the teacher's look of disappointment for not having my school supplies. I wanted to explain why I didn't have them, but I was afraid that it would cause more problems and would be all my fault.

At lunch, the food smelt so good that it made me feel sick. I had no money and didn't understand the process of getting food. I was just lost and confused. After much confusion, I was given a slice of cafeteria pizza and milk. Many of the kids were complaining and throwing it away, but I thought it was delicious! I ate so fast it made my stomach hurt. My tummy always hurt, but I was used to it.

This may be a strange mask to wear but it's called, hunger. It seemed I was always hungry; maybe due to lacking in vitamins and minerals, I don't know, but I'm well-nourished now, for the most part, and more importantly, I hope to nourish the world as well; not just physically, but emotionally and spiritually, leaving it a better place than I found it.

Gandhi couldn't have said it better, "Be the change you want to see in the world."

When Azurdee and I arrived home, neither parent was there, which in my mind meant they were both at dad's shop or that dad took stepmom's body somewhere and would come back for us later. Azure said we had to clean up to make dad happy, so we started doing dishes and laundry. Then, while she was getting dinner ready, I tried lighting a fire in the wood burning stove. For some reason the kindling wouldn't stay lit, so I grabbed a bottle of lighter fluid and squeezed it onto the small, struggling flames. WHOOSH!!! A massive blaze gushed at my face! Screaming hysterically, I jumped up and down, slapping myself frantically trying to put the fire out! My sister shouted, "Flower!" And I froze. All at once, she started laughing because I was indeed NOT

ON FIRE and I looked pretty ridiculous! Realizing I was fine, I joined her chuckles amidst my tears. She hugged me and took over the fire building. And still to this day I've never successfully lit a fire, but I'm fine with that.

Anyway, soon after that, dad and stepmom arrived home drunk, high, and happy. Everything was so surreal. Do these people really live like this? How is this possible?

Azurdee knew their system well and was a Master Teacher of valiance to me.

And then, the mask of pretend solidified itself. Thankfully I can't fake anything anymore. For years I believed in the fake it til you make it motto, but it didn't work. Now I believe in, "Make it happen or die trying!"

Dad took over the cooking and us girls stood beside him. The moment seemed happy and light and he didn't have a shirt on... so, feeling frisky, I called out, "Titty Twister!" and twisted his bare nipple. Instantaneously, his fist went up and I hit the floor! Azure grabbed his arm and screamed, "Dad! She was kidding!" I remained crouched in the corner until he walked away to cool off. Azurdee said, "Fuck Flower! Come here, its ok." And she hugged me. Wow, two hugs in one day. I was on a roll. Haha!

One evening I was playing cards with Christ and our folks were watching a game show on TV and when they started arguing, I went to my room (the trailer). As the fighting progressed, I followed Azurdee toward the house where we saw Christ peering into the bathroom window. He said the bathroom door was locked. Our dad was beating his mom with a baseboard style space heater. Then he shoved her head in the toilet water and bashed her face into the side of it, shouting, "You like that?!" Drunk and debilitated she just moaned. We all screamed and yelled hysterically, banging on the small window, begging him to stop.

I was so scared I don't remember anything else.

As I think back on all of this, it was as if I wasn't really there and this was not my life.

The most revolting thing was hearing them have sex after he'd mutilate her.

Call The Police!

Fortunately, some kind, concerned neighbors moved into the house next door, which I recall us living in temporarily, after a storm caused a tree branch to fall through the roof of the little house.

Anyway, the new family seemed grief stricken that we lived this way and they'd call the police when mayhem broke out. Sadly, the police usually couldn't resolve anything because stepmom would lie and say she fell off her horse or something. When the officials left, dad would scold us; yelling and poking his hard, stubby finger into our chests, as if it were our fault...which of course I assumed it was due to our petrified screams. **This brings us to the mask of guilt/ blame. I've since realized I was never and am never to blame for the actions of anyone else; I'm only accountable for my responses to them. So, I'm determined to do a better job responding to things in order to bring about a much better future for myself and my children. I'm surely a work in progress, but I'm driven by the need to leave a legacy of goodness for generations to come.**

Can't I just save the world with my uniquely loopy and unorthodoxed ways?

Anyway, back to the neighbors, they were good people. One day the mom inquired about our mother and then helped us mail her a secret letter! Azure had an impeccable memory of addresses and phone numbers, so she knew where to send it in hopes that mom would get it. I felt terrible for what I wrote in my letter. It seemed like such a bad thing to say, but I had to do it because this was most likely going to be my only chance. "Dear Mom, I don't like it here. I want to come home." Love Flower.

Waiting for mom's reply felt like an eternity. When it finally came, we rushed to open it. Crouched on the steps between our place and the neighbors and riddled with anticipation to discover the private location we'd be sneaking off to meet her, Azure read aloud. Her voice trembled and the paper shook, "Dear girls, I love you so much, but I can't come get you. I'm living in a car with my boyfriend and I have no room for you."

And this was the moment that I placed the God of All Masks upon my little face;

WORTHLESS!

But now I say to myself, "Silly girl, you're not worthless. In fact, NOTHING could be further from the truth! You're a priceless treasure with value far above that of any gem. You're a miracle. Your very breath puts stars in orbit."

Think back on your life. Have lies shaped your beliefs?

<u>THE TRUTH IS YOU'RE PRECIOUS BEYOND MEASURE!</u>

YOU'RE WORTH BEING RESCUED, EVEN IF YOU HAVE TO SAVE YOURSELF!

THAT'S THE TRUTH! BELIEVE IT!

Chapter 6

Were You Born in a Barn?
No, But I Was Raised in One.

Again, times were tough and money was tight, so the Landlord let us move into an old, unused Turkey Barn. Summer was hot and sweaty. Winter was icy cold. Our bedroom trailer became the family's kitchen and bathroom and us girls moved into a large tent. Christ still had the camper shell, and tarps were hung to create a makeshift master bedroom for the grownups, which doubled as a living room where us kids sat on the dirt ground to watch TV; one night, while hanging out in there eating dessert, Azure said, "Flower, smell this!" Totally engrossed in the TV show, I leaned over without thinking and smelt the most gagacious odor in my life and Azuredee was in hysterics! "I farted in it!" she exclaimed, as she showed me her empty ice-cream cup. Ugh...it made my eyes water. "Eww!" I contested, and we roared with laughter. She told me in 2009, that she'd been storing that fart patiently throughout the show, just waiting to share it with me! Thanks Azure, that's just great.

Other journeys and mishaps in the barn included hanging a tire swing from one of the beams. It was all fun and games until the rope broke and I went soaring through the air, crashing in the corner. I was mad at myself because I had a feeling it would break, but I blamed my sister, because she was the one pushing me. There was also a lizard that lived in the barn. It rarely ever had a tail, probably from the cats. Whenever we tried to catch him he bit us, opposed to running. And then, there was my ultimate cow dare. I challenged myself to pet one of the cattle that wandered on the property. I noticed a curious one watching me, so I chose him. I had to move very slowly because if I went too fast he'd start to leave. As I inched my way toward him, my heart pounded. I tried not to stare at him because when I did, he scuffed the earth and rattled his head. Every once in awhile I stopped and looked around acting as if I didn't notice him. Then I hummed peaceful tunes and started toward him. He stared intently as I approached. By the time I was close enough to touch him, he let out a huff. I reached out, slowly and gently petting his forehead and thanking him. He was much taller than me, and had horns breaking through on his forehead. They were covered in a baby fine hair, but it wasn't as soft as it looked. For a moment we stood captivated by the stillness, and we were the same; scared and brave.

Eventually another trailer came into the barn to be the living room and master bedroom for dad and stepmom. As I'm sure you can imagine, it was soon christened with blood. For some reason, living in the turkey barn is where I remember stepmom instigating a lot of fights, which really confused me. She'd become so belligerent with dad, even to the point of attacking him! Maybe she was finally fighting back or maybe she'd always been this way, I'm not sure. All I know is that it was her blood staining the walls. Dad smashed her face into a door jam, but one of the worst times was when he stomped on her face with cowboy boots on while she lay on the ground scratching at his feet. **The sound**

was sickening. I still can't allow myself to fully revisit this memory, nor do I ever wish to.

I hated life, and began to despise myself. Once I was going through some pictures and every time I found one that I thought I looked good in, I said to myself, "No! You're ugly!" And then I either tore it up, or cut myself out of it. At first it hurt my feelings to do this, but then it became a habit; so did destroying any works of art I'd created. Eventually I was so disgusted with my looks that I tried scrubbing my face with a pumice stone to make my face and especially my nose smaller. Afterwards my face burned like crazy and I looked like Rudolph!

Christ had grown taller and more scraggly looking. His facial hair was a patchy mess, his teeth were grossly stained and crooked, and his glasses were held together in 2 places with black electrical tape, not to mention his sloppy gait, poor posture, dirty clothes and uncut hair all made him seem unapproachable. His taste in music had evolved too. He was really into the rock band Deep Purple, which I hated for years because of him. But while working on this book, it occurred to me that they likely aided in my rescue, so I gave them another listen. This time with renewed perspective and a grateful heart and I actually think they're pretty amazing. Anyway, I hadn't been in his 'room' for a long time. He had the music blaring and convinced me to come in. Skeptically, I climbed in and looked around, pretending not to hear him say, "Close the door." I was instantly aware of his intentions when I saw dirty magazines opened and sprawled about. Within moments my sister was there demanding I get out! She looked pissed, rightfully assuming the worst and told me to go away. With heightened curiosity from those magazines, I wandered to the outhouse where I'd seen some of them before but never opened them. As I flipped through the pages, I felt tickling sensations in my privates and the instinctive urge to rub myself. For the next couple of years, I viewed porn and masturbated fairly regularly.

I became obsessed with the magazines and they taught me well.

Sadly, a child this age should be enjoying pillow fights and innocent sleepovers; not confused by uncontrollable sexual urges when she's out lizard hunting! Orgasms are amazing, but it's important for each individual to explore them in their own time and in their own way. **Sexuality is an aspect of life boasting enough challenges of its own without any additives! Besides, just because something feels good, doesn't mean it is good. Sane and honorable judgements are critical in this arena because it really fucks with a person when it's in disarray.**

Chapter 7

My Apologies...

If you feel uncomfortable by the contents of this book, saddened, overwhelmed, ashamed, appalled, grossed out, enraged by the injustice of it; or even if you feel strangely stimulated or curiously aroused; whatever the emotion is that you're feeling, relax, it's ok, it means you're human. If you're reminded of someone or something in your past or present; whether you were a victim, perpetrator, innocent bystander, or one who turned a blind eye, let the emotions move you. If you feel like crying, then cry and let it move you to have compassion for yourself and others. Feel angry? Let the anger move you to climb out of whatever pity pot you may be in. But be careful! Don't let anger lead you to folly. Use its force to motivate you to make a positive difference, but not to pursue evil. Use wisdom and seek counsel as needed. Especially when countering negative emotions. There's balance in everything. We need to set the thermostat of our emotions and this takes time to master and is best accomplished by surrounding yourself with good examples.

Our feelings are meant to guide us, it's their purpose. We can't control the fact that we have them any more than we can control our bodily functions, but we can control how we respond to them. I believe we can also develop the power and authority to set the scale of our emotional thermostat; to set the balance of our "self". After all, if we're going to be held accountable for our actions then we'd better have access to the control center! Right? If this seems impossible to you, or difficult to grasp, be patient with yourself. It's a journey. Enjoy the ride and remember; nobody's perfect. We all shit our pants sometimes and our emotional thermostats go a little wonky and straight up OUT OF WHACK! But, out of whack should NEVER BE THE NORM!

The ultimate goal in life, (in my opinion), is goodness from the inside-out. I apologize if you're offended at how I'm choosing to bring my bag of good into the world, but I believe exposing darkness for what it is, regardless of the worker of it, (me included), is the best way to combat it; to shine a light on the ugly core and clean it out. I agree wholeheartedly with Kate Northrup's mother who said, "You have to feel it to heal it." quoted from Kate Northrup's book, Money, A Love Story.

Let's imagine for a moment that you're helping someone out of a ditch; in this case, that someone is you. It's time to be your own hero! After all, no one knows what you need, better than you. And if you don't know right now, that's ok; you've just temporarily lost connection with your truest self. It'll take time to recover it. It's taken me years to come full circle, recalling who I am. Like I said before, it's a journey. Enjoy it, don't rush.

<u>And Remember!</u>
<u>Let goodness fill you up to overflowing; even if only in your mind, in fact, especially there.</u>

The more you value yourself in an honest way, the better you'll be to yourself and to others. And the less foul treatment you'll put up with and put out into the world.

A note of caution: If you're like me, you'll want to avoid assessing your net worth while trying to establish your self-worth because by net worth standards, I'm in the negative and it's pretty depressing. So, I decided to focus ALL MY WORTH on the things that are most important to me, relationships. Including the one I have with myself.

If you're still offended, and this book isn't benefiting you at all, please stop reading and burn it.

Now, back to those dirty magazines...I vividly remember seeing an issue with a lady riding nude on horseback. She seemed so naturally glamorous that of course I had to try it when no one was home. I'm not sure if it was my instinctive, yet subtle fear of horses, or my overall nervousness in anticipation of the experience, but the horse was stirred and antsy. She was a mature, white, Arabian beauty with a gentle nature and a fiery spirit. I placed only the saddle pad on her back and just before mounting, I took off my clothes and imagined we'd gallivant under the warm, summer sun. But when I hopped on, she was so eager to take off, that after some awkward attempts at trying to control her and be sexy, I jumped off, got dressed and we went for a run. I let her go wherever she wanted and we ended up on top of a mountain! Noticing the sun was about to set, I attempted to guide her down the mountainside and nearly toppled over her! In a panic, I leaned forward to embrace her, but she tensed as though ready to dart, so I loosened the grip of my legs and held tight to her mane. We became as one as she stumbled over the rough terrain. I felt her pounding heart and was certain she felt mine.

Chapter 8

Vertigo

At school, some girls showed me how to do a backward spin on the parallel bars and for some reason, I did exactly what they said NOT TO DO! I threw my head back, rather than keeping it tucked in and I slammed the back of my head into the other bar. I blacked out and hit the ground. When I came to, they were walking me to the office saying, "Oh my god! Look at her eyes!" To this day I have no idea what my eyes were doing. I couldn't see a thing, maybe they fell out! Next thing I knew, I woke up to staff questioning me, "What's today? Do you know your name?" At first I just gave a blank stare…Maybe I broke my brain, I thought, because I wasn't sure what they meant by all these things. In fact, I didn't even know I could speak. It took a moment to gather my senses and it felt strange to feel my voice come from my throat.

"Where else would it come from, my ass?"
Only on special occasions, right?

One day while playing tag at school, I ran up the steps of a tall metal slide and jumped from the top, pushing myself off the side rails with such velocity that I missed landing on the slide completely and hit the ground landing flat on my back! Again, I woke up in the office; this time overhearing the staff discussing the inability to reach my parents and whether to call for an ambulance. Finally my parents arrived and were clearly not happy for the drama I'd caused. It just occurred to me that this was the first time I ever experienced vertigo. I've suffered from it off and on over the years, but never knew where it originated…Hmm, reflection is a beautiful thing.

I remember having a few boyfriends; some nice, others mean, but all cute. For some reason, one day after school, a few of us kids were hanging around the empty campus. We played on the swings and my sister kept urging me to kiss the boy I liked. It made me uncomfortable because I'd never thought about kissing before, so I told her, "No! You do it!" Even though I really didn't want her to and part of me burned with envy just wondering if she would. Strangely, I do recall wanting to see his penis, but I was definitely not interested in kissing. After a while, we sat by the water fountain and the boy I liked started acting very disturbed. He was angry and upset about an unpleasant situation between his parents who were separated. I wondered if his life was like mine, but I didn't say anything.

Another boyfriend had been sort of nice to me, but he always gave me Indian burns and did things to hurt me. Then there was a boy I liked whose sister said he like me back, but he was too shy to make or accept any advances. Looking back, it seemed I was always seeking some secretive, deviant adventures. And lastly, there was the boy I always played with and who was always nice to me, but I never thought of him as the boyfriend type, though later in life someone reminded me of him and I pursued some naughty adventure with him, as you'll soon see.

Hungry and Hallucinating

Still living in the Turkey Barn, food was miniscule, so dad drove behind a local grocery store and sent us 3 "scouts" into the trash bins. I hated this degrading practice with passion but acted like it was so fucking cool just to keep dad from getting mad. It seemed I'd do anything to keep the peace…anything. For years as an adult, I thought of myself as a peacekeeper, but once again the beauty of hindsight revealed truth; I was just afraid to be myself, because in doing so, I may hurt or upset someone. Thank God those days are over! I wish I'd had the courage to tell dad, "No way! You do it." I think I'm a fairly understanding person and probably would've responded better had he explained the situation, instead of just throwing me into it.

One night when our parents were away, we made some 'trash food' for dinner and I got severely ill from eating the meat before it was fully cooked. Azure tried to warn me, but stepdad and I use to eat raw hamburger all the time; well, until we saw a TV show teaching all the bad things about it, but I was so hungry I just couldn't resist. Not long after eating it, I lay scorched with fever, trembling as if I were freezing to death. As hot air from a small heater gushed into my face my hallucination began; I was a tiny figurine climbing it's vent rails and suddenly my fingers were bigger than my head! They were huge and throbbing, but somehow they didn't hurt. My sister kept checking on me and in my lucid moments, I worried that Christ would come in. Flashback! Oh my goodness! I just realized that prior to feeling sick I had smashed my fingers while curiously tinkering with a hatch on back of the trailer. That's why they were throbbing!

Chapter 9

Love and Hate

For the life of me, I can't recall the order of the anarchy, due to being sent to live here and there, and back and forth so many times that it's just going to come out as sporadically as it spins in my head.

It seemed step mom never really liked us. Maybe she felt we were the cause of their fights, and maybe we were. I don't know. Regardless, I hated seeing her suffer so much. By the way, I later learned that the reason he choked her was for putting sugar in the mashed potatoes...because that's a logical reason to try and kill someone...WTF?!?!

It seemed we always had pets, which was nice; dogs, cats, horses, chickens, rabbits, (cattle on the ranch, though not ours), hamsters, rats, snakes and lizards that we caught, and maybe a fish for a day. I recall the time that one of our puppy's killed one of the hens. Dad beat that poor dog profusely and **I hated him.** Everyone was yelling at him to stop and Azurdee was hitting him and the puppy started limping away and then he shot it! Dad! Why must you be so angry? I hate revising this book, because it makes me relive these painful things, but somehow I know that a deeper healing takes place each time. Miraculously, the pup survived. He was later found bleeding in dad's sock basket with the flesh ripped off its shoulder from the gunshot. I was so afraid he'd be beat again or killed, but to my surprise, they bandaged him up.

Another calm and peaceful evening, Dad & Azure were in the kitchen trailer making dinner, I was on my way to join them when I saw stepmom limping along in that direction, using a shotgun rifle as her cane. She was cursing under her breath in Italian, as she often did. I rushed in and whispered a warning to Azurdee who tried convincing dad not to overreact, but to no avail. Dinner was abandoned and anguish ensued...all because of me and my big mouth. As Azure and I fled for safety, a gunshot pierced the night and silenced the echoing commotion. We ran to the trailer with the dogs and were welcomed in for the night. The next morning when Azure tried to wake me, I assured her I wouldn't oversleep and miss my bus. Later when I awoke, I realized I had to stop at home for my backpack and hopefully some food...and I suddenly regretted not going with her. As I entered the barn, all I could hear was the beating of my heart and the scurrying of the rats in their cage. As I turned to leave, there stood stepmom leaning on her cane. Her face was shockingly disfigured, worse than I'd ever seen before. She didn't even look human and it was all my fault. Guilty, frightened and wounded for her, I choked out words I'd never even thought to say to her before, "**I love you.**" Then I squeamishly rushed off to school. All day her gruesome image was in my mind and I couldn't focus on anything else. After all, her pain and suffering was all my fault. And now, I take full responsibility. If only I knew then what I know now, I would have helped her escape. Woulda, shoulda, coulda. Maybe those words should be on my tombstone. Oh God, please help me! I'm crying, trembling, I feel like I'm going to pass out. Everything is shaking. If everything was my fault then I must also have the power to make everything all better! Amen!?! This is my fourth and hopefully final revision of this book… it's torture. I have to move on…

For some reason I don't recall ever celebrating birthdays or holidays with them, but I do remember receiving a gift at school from my mom. It was a Miss Piggy stuffed animal. I loved it because it was from mom, but I hated it because I felt like she didn't know me at all since I wasn't a Muppets fan. I ended up giving it away to a friend who collected stuffed animals. And a few years ago, I reconnected with the friend and she still had it!

Once at the grocery store, stepmom saw me looking at an ugly purple barrette and headband set. She must've thought I liked it because she handed it to me and said, "Buon Compleanno," Happy Birthday in Italian. Maybe she didn't hate me, so I wore them the next day.

For some reason, I don't recall holidays either, but I do remember two Halloweens. As a last minute costume dad cut holes in the sides of a large refrigerator box for my arms to stick through and a hole on top for my head. With duct tape he spelled, OUTHOUSE. To be honest, it felt degrading, but at the time, I didn't care. And trust me when I say that plenty of guys asked if they could use me! For the next Halloween I was a dainty little tooth fairy dressed in a short, lacy, opaque dress; in my mind, this costume made up for the humiliation of being an outhouse.

Chapter 10

Peace Break

Ok, I have to take a moment to let you know that although this book is filled with the hideous nature of males in my life, I must let you know that they were merely products of their environments, as I became also. We all have our own special ways of adhering and adapting. I don't blame them, or anyone else for things I went through or the things that happened to me. Instead, I've decided to become responsible for all my incapacities of childhood. As I browse through the experiences of my past, I search for gems; bad circumstances where I could have stood up for myself or someone else. In doing this, I strive to identify various ways I could've made a difference, or at least attempted to make myself be heard. My intention in doing this is NOT to live in regret or dwell on the past, but to understand the power that I had and still have to make a difference in any situation. This personal exercise actually strengthens, empowers and equips me to take authority over my life and cause situations to serve me, rather than me bowing to them. Obviously, it's a work in progress, as am I.

Aside from my supposed father being an angry, hurt and disturbed man, he was also a very funny, generous and caring man that would go to the ends of the earth to help someone, but anger ruined his life. As a family, we frequented many bars growing up and as he got drunk, played pool or danced with the ladies, us girls would take turns asking for money and he'd dish it out left and right; fifty cents and dollar bills. Occasionally he'd say, "I already gave you some." But, we'd just say, "That was my sister." He was also a big jokester (and a name caller which really bothered me). He'd trick or make fun of me just to get a good laugh. Years later I realized that was my impression of God; a jokester wanting to trip me up so he could get a good laugh. On a few occasions, I saw him cry because he hated who he would become and he felt powerless against it. He didn't know he held the key to his own freedom. After stepmom passed away (God rest her weary soul) and dad was pursuing another woman, she saw his violent side and immediately broke up with him. At home, he fell to his knees and beating his chest he cried out, "She may as well be stabbing daggers in my heart!" I stood there awkwardly not knowing what to do. Then the image of stepmom's disfigured face came to mind and I realized how incredibly brave it was for this new woman to think she could stop him! All I could muster up to say to him was, "I'm sorry." And then I shuffled off to visit this mysterious woman. She told me she'd been abused before and decided it would never happen again. I thought she was crazy, but I wanted what she had.

"Dear Father, I love you and I'm sorry. I'm sorry I hated you and I'm sorry that life was such a struggle for you and that you missed out on a lifetime of joy and the exhilaration of love's freedom. The last time I saw you was in the summer of 1993 when my son was born. I'd NEVER seen you so happy! You used up 3 rolls of film taking pictures! Smiling, giggling and tickling the baby, it was like a brand new you! But then you died suddenly 12 days later. I miss you and I forgive you. When I was a kid, I laughed when you called me names, but in reality, I hated it. To hear it once or twice was funny and fitting in the moment, but the repetition of it became injurious and insulting. I'm so very thankful that you never abused me, however, I do believe your influence did me harm, leaving me vulnerable to ghastly attacks on my very soul because you didn't teach me what a beautiful treasure I was and that I should expect others to love, cherish and respect me. A while back, I drove through the hills whence we once lived and I cried for you. I wished you had another chance to set things right, to be grateful and careful with every precious life you held in the palm of your finite hands. I recall what a hard worker you were; an expert in your trade. And thank you for letting me help you in the shop. I wish I knew more about you. I'm saddened by the legacy you left behind as a father, but I'm thankful for the lessons I continue to discover from the treasure box of my past and I'm learning to be grateful for you."

As for my stepbrother; I can't even imagine what life must've been like for him to watch his mother be beaten so severely and it disturbs me to think what he must have had to endure to make him do such things to me and to others. I felt like a martyr, being sacrificed for causes I didn't understand.

"Dear Christ, I'm sorry I hated you. Thanks for playing cards with me and dressing up the cats and dogs in baby clothes after bathing them in the kiddie pool, (well, trying to bathe the cats). I guess you weren't always a creeper, but for the longest time I couldn't stand you. I wish you could've been the big brother I needed you to be...and I wonder if you wanted to be. Before discovering that you'd passed away, I thought I saw you at a gas station. At first I was afraid and locked my door, but then I remembered how you must have suffered as a child too and I decided that I would hug you and tell you I forgive you, but suddenly you were gone. Tears fill my eyes as I think of you...I'm so sorry your life sucked."

Dear stepmom, I'm sorry you were treated so poorly. I wish things could have been better for you. You should've been adored like a princess and admired like a queen. I wish I could've known how you felt about me and I wish us kids could have been more important to you. I wish I wish....I blow wishes in the wind; may you rest in paradise. Love Flower.

As a kid, I talked a lot, (who am I kidding? I still do), but out of fear and not wanting to hurt or upset people, I rarely spoke my truest thoughts. Instead, I just rambled; you know, talk a lot and say nothing at all. I was practically an expert at it. This trait was serving me well, but eventually it bit me in the ass. I learned the hard way that not speaking my mind is like not having a voice (or a mind) at all, so now I'm practicing the art of honest, respectable articulation.

Chapter 11

Surprise!

Out of the blue, a totally unexpected, remarkable, surprise visit came from daddy! The one I originally thought was my dad. He'd won 50k in the lottery and offered to help our dad by taking us girls until he and stepmom could get back on their feet and dad agreed! It was the best thing ever! I hopped in the truck so elated that I forgot to say goodbye! I was like fuck this man, I'm going home! Then as I skipped over to say goodbye, I realized that they were genuinely sad and I immediately felt bad for being so happy.

Living with Daddy was the RITZ and I loved my new life!! He had a nice, big house, he took me shopping at Hollywood Boutiques, let me play on his instruments; drums, keyboard, guitar, harmonica, etc. I loved watching him sing and practice being a rock star.

One day, my eldest sister determined that I needed a training bra, so we told daddy. First, he asked to see them, but when I shied away, he gave me a pencil and instructed me to go place it under one of my breasts. If my booby could hold it, he'd get a bra. I went in the bathroom and watched in the mirror as the pencil fell the floor again and again. My boobies could do no such trick! But I guess he was kidding because my sister later gave me a bra.

At school, I met a wonderful friend with whom I had splendid sleepovers! We even did homework together. I felt so privileged. I just knew my life was going to be wonderful!

There were 4 of us sisters' altogether and it wasn't long before rumors surfaced that mom heard we were all in one place and she was coming to get us. Naturally, I hoped she and daddy would get back together and my thoughts went wild wondering what life would be like. My new friend made me promise I wouldn't leave. When mom arrived, it was the middle of the night and she had a boyfriend, which was daddy's brother. They all argued and my stomach was in knots. Who would get hurt, maimed, killed, and disfigured? Would I have to run away? Thankfully, things settled down and it was agreed that each of us girls could make our own decision. This made me really happy, until I learned that all of my sisters had already said no. My heart was in anguish. "Mom came all this way and no one will go?" **So, against all my intuitions, I went. I even put a smile on my face. After all, this was what I always wanted, right?** My friend was devastated and I felt like I was losing everything good in my life on a chance with mom.

Chapter 12

Independence

As it turned out mom and her beau lived in a small trailer in a town with a population of about 50, yes fifty and they had no room for me, so I was promptly dropped off at my grandparents. When I couldn't stay there, I went to my aunt's, but she was often away at her boyfriend's place. I didn't know how to cook, but I could use a microwave... sort of. One of my favorite things to eat was marshmallow, peanut butter and chocolate melted together, as long as I didn't cook it too long. There was a kind elderly woman who ran a small market from her garage. I'd offer to help her with chores and she'd give me, food, candy or ice-cream in return. Regretfully, I must admit that I also stole some things from her, like candy, soda and, as I got older, cigarettes.

One night, a man came to visit my aunt but she wasn't home. I put on quite a show performing all the bendy movements of the exercise lady on TV. I felt really mature. More importantly, I felt like I was being desired.

It felt good; I'd gotten use to the shame.

One time he took me to his house. He had a family. I met his kind-faced, homely, downtrodden-looking wife and their 3 young unkempt children. For a moment I thought maybe I could live with them, but it turned out their idea was for me to babysit. I remember feeling a sudden spark of jealousy and confusion. Out of nowhere my thoughts went rampant, "She can watch her own damn kids!" But then after seeing her melancholy face and despondent mannerisms, I felt bad for thinking such things and even worse for what I'd done with him. I never did babysit, in fact, I never saw any of them again, not even him.

I guess my new school was ok. The bus rides were hella long, giving me ample time to sleep or find trouble; like the trouble I found myself in with the boy who reminded me of the friend from elementary school. We sat at the back of the bus. At first he tried to stop me. But I persisted as if it were a game and there was a prize to be won. Sadly, mischief seemed to add value to my life; if only I knew then what I know now, that no matter how exhilarating these things were, they were shallow and temporal. Now I seek true meaning am governed by the desire to leave a strong legacy of good.

Eventually mom, her beau and I moved into a small house which was in the same town as my school and I was told to keep an eye on someone. Regrettably, I had half a mind to fondle him!

One day at a cousin's house, I sat with a group of strangers and a glass bong was being passed around. When it came to me, they had to reload it. I didn't want to be called a chicken for taking a small puff, (cuz I hated that), so I let out all my breath and didn't inhale until it was time to take my hit and when I breathed in, I sucked so hard, the entire cherry came up and I even guzzled some disgusting bong water! I certainly accomplished not being called a wimp, but now everyone was mad at me for hogging it! I was so stoned I couldn't function! I felt the urge to panic, but I couldn't even do that. When my mom arrived, I told her how I felt and she said "It's called being stoned honey, just go to bed".

I woke up later that night on the couch. It was dark. As I laid there trying to make sense of my surroundings, I could hear strange noises in the background. Startled at what I saw, I tried to act like I was asleep, but was soon driven by desires I could not control.

Boy Meets Girl

A friend of mine lived nearby and one day before going to visit her, I found my mom's boyfriend's marijuana pipe and smoked some. It was my first time doing it alone. After eating a few cookies, I met up with her and for some reason her cousins were chasing us and shooting at us with pellet guns. It was scary and exciting all at the same time. In the midst of the chaos, my friend and I got separated and I lost my sense of direction. I stood near a tree, straining to hear footsteps and suddenly the taller boy was right in front of me. Startled, I flinched and put my hands up. He grabbed me. I secretly liked him and wanted this. Afterwards, he shoved me to the ground and shot at me as he ran off calling me names, (confirming my less than admirable self esteem). **Thankfully I know now that the expression of others says more about them than it does about me and I get to choose whether or not to receive the impression expressed by them or let it pass by with a blessing.**

On my birthday, I was given a small bottle of Crown Royal in a purple velvet bag. I drank some the next morning before school and despite the fact that it was 30 degrees and snowing, I left home wearing a mini skirt and sandals. The school authorities couldn't reach my family and couldn't get a straight answer out of me regarding who I lived with. So, I was taken to a facility, given warmer clothes and then taken to a foster home. It was a nice place in a pleasant and peaceful mobile home park. The woman inquired of my likes and dislikes as to my tastes in order to make me a sandwich. I kept shrugging awkwardly. I had no idea what she was trying to offer me. I recall it now, sprouts, pastrami, Dijon, etc. It was delicious! Her husband came in and they had a slight dispute. I thought I might have to run away, but it ended quickly and peacefully. I wanted to live here forever. I stayed one night and started a new school, but before lunch I was taken out of class and told that my dad was there to get me. I wanted to die. **My new world imploded before it ever began.** I walked through the corridor feeling trapped, afraid and unable to show any emotion. On the inside I was screaming, banging on windows of my soul! No! Don't let him take me! Doesn't anybody hear me?! I had never been alone with him before and I was scared! Surely he'd kill me! As soon as we stepped outside, shouts greeted me! He wasn't alone! The couple with all the dogs was there and so was Azurdee! Relieved, I greeted them and we all drove away.

Chapter 13

Back on the Ranch

They now lived on a different part of the same ranch. This time a cluster of trailers made up our "house". I think Azurdee was in high school now or living part time with a boyfriend, because she wasn't around as much. Also, I rarely saw Christ anymore and if I remember correctly, he never touched me again.

It seemed like dad and stepmom swapped jail time and lovers. When dad was away, stepmom brought home a hitchhiker and in the morning they were passed out naked on the floor. I don't recall dad bringing women over, but I do remember him taking me places where I'd be outside and overhear them having sex.

I'm not sure why, but one time, dad and I had to sleep in the same bed and I COULD NOT sleep. Every time he moved, I was afraid. He'd never beat or sexually abused me, but still I feared him and I felt safest when he was snoring, but for some reason, I still couldn't sleep...

Oh well, I probably did at school.

To be honest, I'm not sure when this happened, but through a school health screening, it was determined I needed dental work for lots of cavities. Dad actually took me to a dentist, but he was clearly irritated by the inconvenience of it all and demanded that they do all the work in one visit. Throughout my appointment, the dentist kept apologizing to me for being there so long, but I didn't care. I knew that anywhere was better than home.

One summer, our black lab had puppies. They roamed happily on the ranch. I thoroughly enjoyed trying to train them, but then, they got the parvo-virus and were dying rapidly. I felt led to boil turkey neck and innards that I found. I boiled it a long time. Eventually, the bones disintegrated. After it cooled, I used a medical syringe to feed the puppies. Sadly, only one survived. After spending the weekend nursing the puppy, I named him Black Sabbath, but Dad freaked out, so I changed his name to Savage. He was an excellent dog and I had him for several years.

A Vietnam Vet (51/50) now lived in a trailer nearby and I'm not sure how this all came about, but some deal between him and dad went very bad. I came home to chaos and was told to drive the man's car and follow dad in his truck. The man's dog was in the back seat and when I arrived at the location, I got out of the car to see what was going on. The man was standing in a phone booth, most likely calling police, and dad was running toward him, ready to kill. The guy stepped back and bent down to grab a bad-ass machete from his boot; but he was a moment too late. Dad kicked him in the face and he went flying backwards! That night, dad's fury was unleashed on that man! The man's dog was going savage in the car! I wanted to let him out of the car to rescue his owner, but when I reached in through the window to unlock the door, he bit me, so I left him alone. I don't remember the rest of that night, but I saw that man over 10 years later at a church. He was crippled. I wanted to apologize to him for what my father had done, but I was afraid. If he saw me, did he recognize me? If so, was he seeking vendetta or peace?

Chapter 14

Ballistic

Transferred to a new school, again, in the middle of Jr. High, I remember wanting to do well, though it didn't last long. Bouncing through so many schools and homes made it virtually impossible to succeed.

Even my Elective Classes were drudgery. It seemed someone else always came along to do my projects, so I'd just leave. Sadly, I even passed up opportunities I would've enjoyed. I just didn't care and when I tried to care, I couldn't catch up, so it was easier not to care. And before I knew it, I was in trouble again; probably for not turning in homework, wandering around campus during class, dressing inappropriately or flashing my privates... who know? Maybe it was a dare, I'm not sure, but in detention, I stood on the desk and quickly exposed my breasts to my fellow recidivists. The teacher soon returned with the principal who escorted me out and suspended me.

Most people that encountered me would say my appearance was that of a kind, young, innocent looking girl, but what burned beneath my skin was an angry, lovesick twin. I wanted good, and I wanted it real bad, but I didn't know how to attain it. My character was not yet skilled in making the best of things. And so without thought or care I employed suffering on innocent bystanders. Like sneaking into houses, or tearing up someone's mail. I knew it was wrong, but I was clueless as to just how wrong! To prove myself unto my fellow peers and show I wasn't scared. I walked right in the back door of a random house and then out the front where they awaited, gasping in astonishment. It wasn't a big deal to me; after all, I didn't steal anything. I hated who I was, and didn't care for much for anyone else. Thankfully, I met a friend, whose family sort of became my rock, (in fact, I later moved away with them, until my first love's gridlock); more on that later.

Strangely, my mom had come to live on the ranch... I'm not sure how that all came about, but she and the Landlord seemed quite friendly. He even bought me new clothes for my few good grades. He wanted to take pictures of me in the outfits, which was a little awkward; and had mom not been there, I'm sure I would've complied.

One day mom shared a line of cocaine with me and afterwards, I went to my friend's house. Paranoia set in pretty bad. My heart was racing and I could hear crazy things, so I clamored under a desk claiming to hear a battle outside. I thought they were after me; turns out it was just nearby construction. My friend's mother happened to care for drug addicted babies. She questioned me until I confessed. She promptly called my mother and threatened to involve authorities. My mother swore it was only baking soda, but the woman could tell by my eyes, heart rate and behavior that it wasn't. Years later my mother apologized to me and admitted she was scared shitless at the time and wasn't about to fess up to anything.

For some reason I always gave things away; even if I loved them. I think it was to be liked and accepted. I hated myself so much that I needed something for others to like about me, and I found it in giving.

Once I had an awesome mountain bike that I rode almost everywhere, but only had it for a few months because a cute boy said he liked it and I gave it to him, though I never admitted to liking him. the Landlord bought me some groovy knee high moccasins and a girl I'd just met said she loved them, so they became hers and I went barefoot. Another gal liked my leather jacket, but it didn't fit her. It seemed that no matter what the item was, if it was in my power to give it, I gave. Years later, someone pointed out that this was offensive to those who had given me the gifts, so I began to curb this habit and try appreciating my blessings, though it was extremely awkward and I felt like I was doing something wrong; like I was hoarding and not sharing.

At some point I recall the entire family; mom, dad, stepmom, Azurdee, plus our oldest sister, and even the people with the dogs, all going out for pizza to meet mom's new man. It was actually pretty exciting. A genuine night filled with fun and laughter. Then again, I had quite the contact high from everyone else getting stoned in the car before we went into the restaurant. Haha! Azure proved her seniority that night by winning and giving away nearly every stuffed animal from the machine! This restaurant had a stage in the back room where we were seated, so naturally I had to perform....pretending to be a rock star.

And my grand finale; mooning the audience!

Somehow I ended up in High School where I was even more lost academically, socially and emotionally. Days at school were straight up confusion. Within 15 minutes of class, I'd make an excuse to leave and not go back. Sometimes I left unnoticed and other times it involved a dramatic scene of me telling the teacher to fuck off. I feel bad for treating them like that, but at the time I just didn't care. However, I did think Cooking Class would be great, but when I tried to get involved, someone was already doing all the work and strangely, I didn't have the courage to say I wanted to help, so I left.

I usually spent my days walking around town, hanging out by the creek listening to the infamous rock bands of the day (where I met my first love). And sometimes I went on spontaneous adventures with random acquaintances doing whatever dares elicited themselves' to me or those I was with; stealing gas, driving out into nowhere... Sex, drugs, rock and roll; what could be better? Right? Accepting one particular dare got me in a bit of trouble; I was told to have sex with a guy I didn't know, in the shower. I had no idea whose house it was and to my knowledge, no adult was home. A few days later some girls were planning to kick my ass... apparently that guy had a girlfriend. I was scared and wished I could explain that I didn't know, but the truth was, even if I did know, I wouldn't have cared. With a rush of adrenaline, I remembered dad's handy advice, "Never be afraid. No matter how big and tough they look, never be afraid." So, **my fear became my courage** and I decided that I was bigger than all of them put together. Fueled by fear, I charged them, cursing and flailing! To my surprise they all ran into a nearby store. With me on their heels, they scattered in every direction. A store clerk yelled for me to get out. Humored by my ingenious, I gloated away with a smile.

Supposedly a rumor was spread at school that I was gay. I hadn't thought about whether I was or not but I didn't like someone else deciding it for me and I was pissed. I stormed out of class to find who said it and when I confronted her, she just stared at me, which infuriated me and led me to assume she had indeed started it. I was so enraged I hocked a big ol' loogie in her face! I guess bullying was my new problem eliminator. I wanted to pummel her, but at the same time, I didn't want to hurt her. Conflicted by rage and compassion, I ran away, leaving her in the middle of a jeering crowd. For years, I cried about this; I even tried contacting her to apologize.

If only I knew then what I know now; rumors don't define me; my own actions do.

In the midst of the mess called High School, some counselors convinced me to join the California Conservation Corps where I participated in some good works. One day I took a ghetto blaster to a worksite with me and one of the kids started mocking it. I wanted to punch him in the face, but I'd learned from spitting on that girl that I didn't like hurting people; so instead, I began smashing the radio with a hammer. Momentarily it made me feel better, but everyone thought I was crazy.

Eventually, ditching school became the norm and so did missing the bus back home. Midway through the semester, I dropped out completely and stayed away from home for good. The day I decided to leave, I called my mom and told her I wouldn't be back. She said she understood, but wished I'd change my mind. I was promptly reported as a runaway so I had to lay low. There were a few close calls when I stumbled upon dad and mom's new husband out looking for me.

Somehow I was always lucky finding places to crash; in cars, on couches and in someone's garage where I had my first sexual encounter with 2 guys, and another time I woke up with a very sweet guy and still to this day have no idea how I ended up at his apartment in the first place. I was always thankful for people who let me stay the night, but I didn't have money to give them, so I'd either clean their place, or give sexual favors in return, or both.

Maybe subconsciously I was looking for love.

One day an acquaintance picked me up and took me to a motel. We went into the restroom and she opened a sleek black case filled with a rainbow variety of pills. She said I could pick anything, so I chose red. Little did I know, it was ecstasy. She explained that some guys would be joining us and we'd party with them. The only other thing I recall from that night, besides the loud music, is bits and pieces of being thrown around like a rag doll.

One day amidst my wanderings, I called home and Azurdee told me that stepmom had passed away. I was actually relieved for her passing because I knew her suffering was over. I couldn't help but chuckle at the irony of it all; she survived all those horrendous beatings from dad, only to lose her life by her drinking problem that caused cirrhosis of the liver.

Like dad, she didn't know she held the key to her own freedom.

Chapter 15

All I Ever Wanted!

Quite temporarily I moved away with my friend and her family. It seemed like a new life was sure to dawn, but, missing the emotional connection with my boyfriend was something I could not endure, so I moved back to be with him. He was in his 20's and we told people I was 17, although I was only 14. He was a drifter, hitching rides wherever he fancied and working odd jobs. We bounced around in various living conditions, staying in cars, with friends, acquaintances, our parents, and oddly enough, we even moved to the ranch where he worked with my dad and I worked with that mysterious lady who had turned dad away years earlier.

Remember my dog Savage? Well, one night my beau and I were stoned and started playing with a stuffed animal. We put on a little play for Savage who sat watching intently. Then we began a tug of war with the bunny, twisting and pulling until suddenly his head broke off! "Oh my gosh! Poor bunny!" We howled with laughter. The next morning we awoke to a real live rabbit head on the floor! Talk about a WTF moment!

While living with my boyfriend in an apartment with his friend and their new family, I received a call from Azurdee and mom. Azure was crying. She explained that dad was not my father and that his brother was really my dad. At first I wasn't sure which of his brothers she was referring to, but then I remembered the one… When I was very little, there was a young guy fixated on scaring me! He'd put on a mask and hide. Then he'd beckon me sweetly and jump out right in front of me when I got close. He was only 16 when he impregnated my 22 yr old mother who was married to his brother, so he was practically a kid himself when I was young and had a great time harassing me. I met him later in life and he's a wonderful man.

On my 16th birthday, my supposed father, gave me a bizarre gift; a stick horse. He said it was for his first grandchild. What's even more bizarre is that I was pregnant 4 months later.

For a change of pace, my beau and I moved in with my mother and her husband who now lived in a modern day ghost town. I babysat and cleaned houses, though I still couldn't cook more than hot dogs and mac and cheese, and he worked at a nearby burger joint. We were partying a lot and I became so ill that my mom thought I had alcohol poisoning. She took me to the doctor where we discovered I was 4 and-a-half months pregnant! I quit smoking, drinking, drugs; everything!

Lewdness lived its prime. Now it's time to shift the paradigm. Or so I thought.

Chapter 16

Are You My Mother?

The day after finishing the manuscript for this book I had the STRANGEST DREAM! I dreamt that my mother told me she wasn't really my mom, and that her mother was my mom. In the dream I called my grandmother (who's actually passed away), and she solemnly confirmed it. For a moment I was baffled, but then I said to her, "It doesn't matter, as long as we all love each other." When I woke up, I considered the possibility of this being real; after all, my dad did sleep with all but one of my mom's sisters. Maybe he slept with her mother too? Right away I contacted my mom and told her the dream. When I asked if it was true, she said, "Of course honey, I just forgot to tell you."

This is The End of My Ugly
And the beginning of The Journey to My Beauty

Be beautiful, and love always.
Sincerely,
Flower

www.ingramcontent.com/pod-product-compliance
Lightning Source LLC
Chambersburg PA
CBHW030526290526
45786CB00004B/1643